Practical
Low Fat

p^3

This is a P³ Book
This edition published in 2003

P³
Queen Street House
4 Queen Street
Bath BA1 1HE, UK

ISBN: 1-40540-550-3

Printed in China

NOTE

This book uses metric and imperial measurements. Follow the same units
of measurement throughout; do not mix metric and imperial.
All spoon measurements are level: teaspoons are assumed to be 5 ml, and
tablespoons are assumed to be 15 ml. Unless otherwise stated,
milk is assumed to be full fat, eggs and individual vegetables such as potatoes
are medium, and pepper is freshly ground black pepper.

The nutritional information provided for each recipe is per serving or per person.
Optional ingredients, variations or serving suggestions have
not been included in the calculations. The times given for each recipe are an approximate
guide only because the preparation times may differ according to the techniques used by
different people and the cooking times may vary as a result of the type of oven used.

Recipes using raw or very lightly cooked eggs should be
avoided by children, the elderly, pregnant women, convalescents,
and anyone suffering from an illness.

Contents

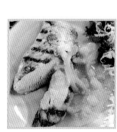

Introduction

Healthy eating means that you can enjoy all of your favourite foods and still keep in great shape. These carefully selected recipes will show you how you can eat nutritious, filling, well-balanced meals, full of flavour and low in fat. Packed full of dishes that are quick and simple to prepare, low-fat cooking provides an array of healthy, delicious dishes for you, your family and your guests to enjoy.

Reducing your fat intake

Reducing the fat content in our diet is very easy and the benefits are myriad. Not only do supermarkets provide a variety of healthy alternatives to full-fat ingredients, such as low-fat dairy products, but the variety of fresh fruit and vegetables available provides excellent sources of essential vitamins. The easiest and quickest way to reduce your fat calorie intake is to change from full-fat milk, and full-fat cream, cheese and yogurt, to a low- or reduced-fat equivalent. Semi-skimmed milk, for example, has all the nutritional benefits of full-fat milk but 10 g/⅓ oz of fat per pint compared with 23 g/¾ oz of fat per pint in full-fat milk.

The benefits of fat

Reducing the level of fat in your diet is synonymous with losing weight. Yet there are many benefits in eating the right types of fat of which many dieters are unaware. It is important to remember that we all need to include a certain amount of fat in our dairy intake to function properly. Essential fatty acids are required in order to build cell membranes and for other vital bodily functions. Our brain tissues, nerve sheaths and bone marrow need fat, and we also need fat to protect organs such as our liver, kidneys and heart.

When is fat bad?

Fat is bad when we consume a high level of it in our diet. Too much fat increases the risk of developing coronary disease, diabetes and even cancer – and, of course, it can lead to obesity. But high-fat diet-related illnesses are not limited to those who are overweight. Nutritionists suggest that we should aim to cut our intake of fat to 27–30 per cent of our total daily calorie intake. If your average daily intake totals 2,000 calories, this will mean eating no more than about 75 g/2¾ oz of fat a day. As a guide, most people consume 40 per cent of their daily calories in the form of fat. However, you should always consult your family doctor if you are being treated for any medical condition before you begin a new regime.

Different types of fat

Fats are made up of a combination of fatty acids and glycerol. Fatty acids consist of a chain of carbon atoms linked to hydrogen atoms. The way these are linked determines whether they are saturated or unsaturated fats, and consequently if they should be avoided or not.

Saturated fats: these are easily recognisable. Saturated fats are solid at room temperature and are mainly found in animal products, such as meat and dairy foods, although some vegetable oils, including palm and coconut oil, contain them. The body has difficulty processing these saturated fats and, as a result, it tends to store them. They increase cholesterol levels in the bloodstream, which can in turn increase the risk of heart disease. It is therefore important to reduce the level of saturated fats in the diet. They should comprise no more than 30 per cent of the total fat intake or no more than nine per cent of the total energy intake.

Unsaturated fats: these are normally liquid or soft at room temperature and are thought to reduce the level of cholesterol in the bloodstream. There are two types of unsaturated fats: monounsaturated and polyunsaturated. The former are mainly found in vegetables, but they also occur in oily fish, such as mackerel. The latter are only found in oily fish and seed oils.

Cooking methods

The way we cook our food is one of the most important factors in ensuring a healthy, low-fat diet. In general, steaming is the best way to cook vegetables to preserve their goodness. Boiling can destroy up to three-quarters of the vitamin C present in green vegetables. This guide will help you choose the healthiest way to cook your dish, while maintaining optimum flavour and colour.

KEY	
	Simplicity level 1–3 (1 easiest, 3 slightly harder)
	Preparation time
	Cooking time

Deep-frying: this is the most fat-rich method of cooking. Yet, surprisingly, deep-frying the food absorbs less fat than shallow-frying. To cut down on fat intake, buy a good-quality, non-stick frying pan because you will need less fat, and use a vegetable oil that is high in polyunsaturates. A good method is to stir-fry food: you require little oil because the food is cooked quickly over a high heat.

Grilling: this is a good alternative to deep-frying, producing a crisp, golden coating while keeping food tender and moist. Ingredients with a delicate texture that can easily dry out, such as white fish or chicken breasts, need brushing with oil. Marinating can reduce the need for oil. Always cook on a rack, so that the fat drains away.

Poaching: this is ideal for foods with a delicate texture or subtle flavour, such as chicken and fish, and it is fat-free. The cooking liquid can make the basis of a nutritious and flavoursome sauce: try alternative liquids such as stock, wine and acidulated water, flavoured with herbs and vegetables.

Steaming: this is also fat-free and is becoming a popular method of cooking meat, fish, chicken and vegetables. Ingredients maintain their colour, flavour and texture, and fewer nutrients are leached out. An additional advantage is that when meat is steamed, the fat melts and drips into the cooking liquid – this should not then be used for gravy.

Braising and stewing: slow-cooking techniques produce succulent dishes that are especially welcome in winter. Trim all visible fat from the meat and always remove the skin from the chicken.

Roasting: fat is an integral part of this cooking technique and without it meat or fish would dry out. Try standing meat on a rack over a roasting tray so that the fat drains off. Do not use the meat juices for gravy.

Baking: many dishes are fat-free. Foil-wrapped parcels of meat or fish are always delicious. Add fruit juice or wine instead of oil or butter for a moist texture.

Microwave: food cooked in this way rarely requires additional fat.

Chicken & Leek Soup

This satisfying soup may be served as a main course. Add rice and peppers to make it even more hearty, and colourful.

NUTRITIONAL INFORMATION

Calories ....183 Sugar 4g
Protein ....21g Fat 9g
Carbohydrate ....4g Saturates 5g

 5 mins   1¹⁄₄ hrs

SERVES 4–6

I N G R E D I E N T S

2 tbsp butter

350 g/12 oz leeks

350 g/12 oz boneless chicken

1.2 litres/2 pints chicken stock

1 bouquet garni

8 stoned prunes, halved

salt and white pepper

300 g/10½ oz cooked rice and diced
  peppers (optional)

1 Melt the butter in a large saucepan.
  Trim the leeks and cut into 2.5-cm/
1-inch pieces.

2 Add the chicken and leeks to the
  saucepan and cook for 8 minutes.

3 Next add the chicken stock and
  bouquet garni and stir together well.

4 Season the mixture well with salt and
  freshly ground pepper to taste.

5 Bring the soup to the boil, then
  simmer for 45 minutes.

6 Add the stoned prunes to the
  saucepan, with the cooked rice and
diced peppers if using, and simmer for
about 20 minutes.

7 Remove the soup from the heat. Lift
  out the bouquet garni and discard.
Serve the soup immediately.

VARIATION

Instead of the bouquet garni,
you can use a bunch of fresh
mixed herbs, tied together with
string. Choose herbs such as
parsley, thyme and rosemary.

Vegetables with Tahini Dip

This tasty dip is great for livening up simply cooked vegetables. Varying the vegetables according to the season adds interest to the dish.

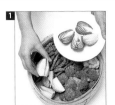

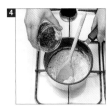

NUTRITIONAL INFORMATION

Calories 126	Sugars 7g	
Protein 11g	Fat 6g	
Carbohydrate 8g	Saturates 1g	

5 mins   20 mins

SERVES 4

INGREDIENTS

225 g/8 oz small broccoli florets

225 g/8 oz small cauliflower florets

225 g/8 oz asparagus, cut into 5-cm/ 2-inch lengths

2 small red onions, cut into quarters

1 tbsp lime juice

2 tsp toasted sesame seeds

1 tbsp chopped fresh chives, to garnish

HOT TAHINI & GARLIC DIP

1 tsp sunflower oil

2 garlic cloves, crushed

½–1 tsp chilli powder

2 tsp tahini (sesame seed paste)

150 ml/5 fl oz low-fat natural fromage frais

2 tbsp chopped fresh chives

salt and pepper

1 Line the base of a steamer with baking paper and arrange the broccoli florets, cauliflower florets, asparagus and onion pieces on top.

2 Bring a wok or large saucepan of water to the boil and place the steamer on top. Sprinkle the vegetables with lime juice and steam them for 10 minutes or until they are just tender.

3 To make the dip, heat the oil in a small, non-stick pan, add the garlic, chilli powder and seasoning and cook gently for 2–3 minutes until the garlic is softened.

4 Remove the pan from the heat and stir in the tahini and fromage frais. Return the pan to the heat and cook gently for 1–2 minutes, without bringing to the boil. Stir in the chives.

5 Remove the vegetables from the steamer and place on a warmed serving platter. Sprinkle over the toasted sesame seeds and garnish with chopped fresh chives. Serve with the hot dip.

Bruschetta

Traditionally, this Italian savoury is enriched with olive oil. Here, sun-dried tomatoes are a good substitute and only a little oil is used.

NUTRITIONAL INFORMATION

Calories 178   Sugars 2g
Protein ....8g   Fat 6g
Carbohydrate ...24g   Saturates 2g

🥄 45 mins   🕐 5 mins

SERVES 4

INGREDIENTS

60 g/2¼ dry-pack sun-dried tomatoes

300 ml/10 fl oz boiling water

35-cm/14-inch long granary or wholemeal stick of French bread

1 large garlic clove, halved

25 g/1 oz stoned black olives in brine, drained and cut into quarters

2 tsp olive oil

2 tbsp chopped fresh basil

40 g/1½ oz low-fat mozzarella cheese, grated

salt and pepper

fresh basil leaves, to garnish

1 Place the sun-dried tomatoes in a heatproof bowl and pour over the boiling water.

2 Set aside for 30 minutes to soften. Drain well and pat dry with kitchen paper. Slice into thin strips and set aside.

3 Trim and discard the ends from the bread and cut into 12 slices. Arrange on a grill rack and place under a preheated hot grill. Cook for 1–2 minutes on each side until lightly golden.

4 Rub both sides of each piece of bread with the cut sides of the garlic. Top with strips of sun-dried tomato and the olives.

5 Brush lightly with olive oil and season well. Sprinkle over the basil and mozzarella and return to the grill for 1–2 minutes until the cheese is melted and bubbling.

6 Transfer to a warmed serving platter and garnish with fresh basil leaves.

COOK'S TIP

If you use sun-dried tomatoes packed in oil, drain them, rinse well in warm water and drain again on kitchen paper to remove as much oil as possible. Sun-dried tomatoes give a rich, full flavour to this dish, but thinly sliced fresh tomatoes can be used instead.

Mixed Leaf Salad

Make this attractive salad with as many varieties of salad leaves and edible flowers as you can find to give an unusual effect.

NUTRITIONAL INFORMATION

Calories 51	Sugars 0.1g
Protein 0.1g	Fat 6g
Carbohydrate 1g	Saturates 1g

5 mins   0 mins

SERVES 4

INGREDIENTS

½ head frisée

½ head feuille de chêne or quattro stagione

few leaves of radicchio

1 head chicory

25 g/1 oz rocket

few sprigs fresh basil or flat-leaved parsley

edible flowers, to garnish (optional)

FRENCH DRESSING

1 tbsp white wine vinegar

pinch of sugar

½ tsp Dijon mustard

3 tbsp extra-virgin olive oil

salt and pepper

1 Tear the frisée, feuille de chêne and radicchio into pieces. Place the salad leaves in a large serving bowl or individual bowls if you prefer.

2 Cut the chicory into diagonal slices and add to the bowl with the rocket leaves, and basil or parsley.

3 To make the dressing, beat the vinegar, sugar and mustard in a small bowl until the sugar has dissolved. Gradually beat in the olive oil until creamy and thoroughly mixed. Season to taste with salt and pepper.

4 Pour the dressing over the salad and toss thoroughly. Sprinkle a mixture of edible flowers over the top, if using. Serve.

COOK'S TIP

Violas, rock geraniums, nasturtiums, chive flowers and pot marigolds add vibrant colours and a sweet flavour to any salad. Use as a centrepiece at a dinner party, or to liven up a simple everyday meal.

Pasta Provençale

A combination of vegetables tossed in a tomato dressing, served on a bed of assorted salad leaves, makes an appetising meal.

NUTRITIONAL INFORMATION

Calories 197   Sugars 5g
Protein ....10g   Fat 5g
Carbohydrate ...30g   Saturates 1g

10 mins   15 mins

SERVES 4

I N G R E D I E N T S

225 g/8 oz penne

1 tbsp olive oil

25 g/1 oz stoned black olives, drained and chopped

25 g/1 oz dry-pack sun-dried tomatoes, soaked, drained and chopped

400 g/14 oz canned artichoke hearts, drained and halved

115 g/4 oz baby courgettes, trimmed and sliced

115 g/4 oz baby plum tomatoes, halved

100 g/3½ oz assorted young salad leaves

salt and pepper

shredded basil leaves, to garnish

D R E S S I N G

4 tbsp passata

2 tbsp low-fat natural yogurt

1 tbsp unsweetened orange juice

1 small bunch fresh basil, shredded

1 Cook the penne in a saucepan of boiling water according to the directions on the packet. Do not overcook – it should be tender but still firm to the bite. Drain well and return to the pan.

2 Stir in the olive oil, olives and sun-dried tomatoes. Season with salt and pepper. Leave to cool.

3 Mix the artichokes, courgettes and plum tomatoes into the cooked pasta. Arrange the salad leaves in a serving bowl.

4 To make the dressing, mix all the ingredients together and toss into the vegetables and pasta.

5 Spoon the pasta on top of the salad leaves and garnish with shredded basil leaves.

Oriental Vegetable Noodles

This delicious dish has a mild, nutty flavour from the peanut butter and dry-roasted peanuts.

NUTRITIONAL INFORMATION

Calories . . . . . . .193 Sugars 5g
Protein . . . . .7g Fat 12g
Carbohydrate . . .14g Saturates 2g

🕒 10 mins   🕑 15 mins

SERVES 4

I N G R E D I E N T S

175 g/6 oz green thread noodles or
   multicoloured spaghetti

1 tsp sesame oil

2 tbsp crunchy peanut butter

2 tbsp light soy sauce

1 tbsp white wine vinegar

1 tsp clear honey

125 g/4½ oz daikon, grated

125 g/4½ oz carrot, grated

125 g/4½ oz cucumber, finely shredded

1 bunch spring onions, finely shredded

1 tbsp dry-roasted peanuts, crushed

T O   G A R N I S H

carrot flowers

spring onion tassels

1 Bring a large pan of water to the boil, add the noodles or spaghetti and cook according to the packet instructions. Drain well and rinse in cold water. Leave in a bowl of cold water until required.

2 To make the peanut butter sauce, put the sesame oil, peanut butter, soy sauce, vinegar and honey into a small, screw-top jar. Seal and then shake well to mix thoroughly.

3 Drain the noodles or spaghetti well, place in a large serving bowl and mix in half of the peanut sauce.

4 Using 2 forks, toss in the grated daikon and carrot, then add the shredded cucumber and spring onions. Sprinkle over the crushed dry-roasted peanuts and garnish with carrot flowers and spring onion tassels. Serve the noodles with the remaining peanut sauce.

COOK'S TIP

There are many varieties of Oriental noodles available from Oriental markets, delicatessens and supermarkets. Try rice noodles, which contain very little fat and require little cooking; usually soaking in boiling water is sufficient.

Chargrilled Vegetables

This medley of peppers, courgette, aubergines and red onions can be served on its own or as an unusual side dish.

NUTRITIONAL INFORMATION

Calories	66	Sugars	.........7g
Protein	.........2g	Fat	..........3g
Carbohydrate	....7g	Saturates	.....0.5g

15 mins   15 mins

SERVES 4

INGREDIENTS

1 large red pepper

1 large green pepper

1 large orange pepper

1 large courgette

4 baby aubergines

2 medium red onions

2 tbsp lemon juice

1 tbsp olive oil

1 garlic clove, crushed

1 tbsp chopped fresh rosemary or 1 tsp dried rosemary

salt and pepper

TO SERVE

freshly cooked cracked wheat

tomato and olive relish

1 Halve and deseed the peppers and cut into even-sized pieces, about 2.5 cm/1 inch wide.

2 Trim the courgette, cut in half lengthways and then slice into 2.5-cm/1-inch pieces. Place the peppers and courgette in a large bowl.

3 Trim the aubergines and cut them into quarters lengthways. Peel the onions, then cut each of them into 8 even-sized wedges. Add the aubergines and onions to the peppers and courgette.

4 In a small bowl, whisk the lemon juice with the olive oil, garlic and rosemary. Season to taste with salt and pepper. Pour the mixture over the vegetables and stir to coat evenly.

5 Thread the vegetables onto 8 metal or presoaked wooden skewers. Arrange the kebabs on the grill rack and cook under a preheated grill, turning frequently, for about 10–12 minutes until the vegetables are lightly charred and just softened. Alternatively, cook the kebabs on a barbecue over hot coals, turning frequently, for about 8–10 minutes until softened and beginning to char.

6 Remove the vegetable kebabs from the heat and serve immediately with freshly cooked cracked wheat and a tomato and olive relish.

Salmon Yakitori

The Japanese sauce used here combines well with salmon, although it is usually served with chicken.

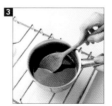

NUTRITIONAL INFORMATION

Calories	...247	Sugars	...10g
Protein	...19g	Fat	...11g
Carbohydrate	...12g	Saturates	...2g

 20 mins   15 mins

SERVES 4

I N G R E D I E N T S

350 g/12 oz chunky salmon fillet

8 baby leeks

Y A K I T O R I   S A U C E

5 tbsp light soy sauce

5 tbsp fish stock

2 tbsp caster sugar

5 tbsp dry white wine

3 tbsp sweet sherry

1 garlic clove, crushed

1 Skin the salmon and cut the flesh into 5-cm/2-inch chunks. Trim the leeks and cut them into 5-cm/2-inch lengths.

2 Thread the salmon and leeks alternately onto 8 presoaked wooden skewers. Leave to chill until required.

3 To make the sauce, place all of the ingredients in a small pan and then heat gently, stirring constantly, until the sugar has dissolved.

4 Bring to the boil, then lower the heat and simmer for 2 minutes. Strain the sauce through a fine sieve and leave to cool until required.

5 Pour one-third of the sauce into a dish. Set aside to serve with the kebabs.

6 Brush plenty of the remaining sauce over the kebabs and place directly on the barbecue. Alternatively, if preferred, place a sheet of oiled kitchen foil on the barbecue and place the salmon on that.

7 Cook the salmon and leek kebabs over hot coals, turning once, for 10 minutes or until cooked through. Using a brush, baste frequently with the remaining sauce during cooking in order to prevent the fish and vegetables from drying out.

8 Transfer the kebabs to a large serving platter and serve with a small bowl of the reserved sauce for dipping.

Fragrant Tuna Steaks

Fresh tuna steaks are very meaty – they have a firm texture, yet the flesh is succulent. Tuna is rich in valuable omega-3 oils.

NUTRITIONAL INFORMATION

Calories	239	Sugars	.......0.1g
Protein	........42g	Fat	..........8g
Carbohydrate	...0.5g	Saturates	......2g

15 mins   15 mins

SERVES 4

INGREDIENTS

4 tuna steaks, about 175 g/6 oz each

½ tsp finely grated lime zest

1 garlic clove, crushed

2 tsp olive oil

1 tsp ground cumin

1 tsp ground coriander

1 tbsp lime juice

pepper

fresh coriander, to garnish

TO SERVE

avocado relish (see Cook's Tip)

tomato wedges

lime wedges

COOK'S TIP

For the avocado relish, peel, stone and chop a small, ripe avocado. Mix in 1 tablespoon lime juice, 1 tablespoon chopped fresh coriander, 1 finely chopped small red onion and some chopped mango or tomato. Season to taste.

1 Trim the skin from the tuna steaks, rinse the fish and pat dry on absorbent kitchen paper.

2 In a small bowl, combine the grated lime zest, garlic, olive oil, cumin and ground coriander. Season with pepper to taste. Mix to make a paste.

3 Spread the paste thinly on both sides of the tuna. Heat a non-stick, ridged

grill pan until hot and press the tuna steaks into it to sear them. Lower the heat and cook for 5 minutes. Turn the fish over and cook for another 4–5 minutes until cooked through. Drain on kitchen paper and transfer to a warmed serving plate.

4 Sprinkle the lime juice over the fish and garnish with fresh coriander. Serve immediately with avocado relish, and tomato and lime wedges.

Plaice with Mushrooms

The moist texture of grilled fish is complemented by the texture of the mushrooms in this dish.

NUTRITIONAL INFORMATION

Calories	243	Sugars	.........2g
Protein	........30g	Fat	..........13g
Carbohydrate	....2g	Saturates	......3g

10 mins   20 mins

SERVES 4

I N G R E D I E N T S

4 white-skinned plaice fillets, about
    150 g/5½ oz each

2 tbsp lime juice

90 g/3¼ oz low-fat spread

300 g/10½ oz mixed small mushrooms such
    as button, oyster, shiitake, chanterelle or
    morel, sliced or cut into quarters

4 tomatoes, skinned, deseeded and chopped

celery salt and pepper

fresh basil leaves, to garnish

fresh mixed salad, to serve

1 Line a grill rack with baking paper and then arrange the plaice fillets on top.

2 Sprinkle over the lime juice and season with celery salt and pepper.

3 Place under a preheated moderate grill and cook for approximately 7–8 minutes, without turning, until just cooked. Keep warm.

4 Meanwhile, gently melt the low-fat spread in a non-stick frying pan, add the mushrooms and cook for 4–5 minutes over a low heat until cooked through.

5 Gently heat the chopped tomatoes in a small saucepan.

6 Spoon the cooked mushrooms, with any pan juices, and the tomatoes over the plaice.

7 Garnish the grilled plaice with the basil leaves and serve with a fresh mixed salad.

COOK'S TIP

Mushrooms are ideal in a low-fat diet because they are packed full of flavour and contain no fat. 'Meatier' types of mushroom, such as chestnut, will take slightly longer to cook.

Scallop Skewers

This delicious scallop dish combines the light, citrus flavour of limes and lemon grass with the heat of the fiery chilli.

NUTRITIONAL INFORMATION

Calories 182   Sugars 0g
Protein . . . . .29g   Fat 7g
Carbohydrate . . . .0g   Saturates 1g

30 mins   10 mins

SERVES 4

I N G R E D I E N T S

juice and grated zest of 2 limes

2 garlic cloves, crushed

2 tbsp finely chopped lemon grass or
   1 tbsp lemon juice

1 green chilli, deseeded and chopped

16 scallops, with corals

2 limes, each cut into 8 segments

2 tbsp sunflower oil

1 tbsp lemon juice

salt and pepper

T O   S E R V E

60 g/2¼ oz rocket

200 g/7 oz mixed salad leaves

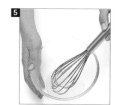

1   Soak 8 skewers in warm water for at least 10 minutes before you use them to prevent the food from sticking.

2   Grind the lime juice and zest, garlic, lemon grass and chilli to a paste in a pestle and mortar or spice grinder.

3   Thread 2 scallops onto each of the soaked skewers. Alternate the scallops with the lime segments.

4   Cover the ends of the skewers with foil to prevent them from burning.

5   For the dressing, whisk together the oil, lemon juice, and salt and pepper.

6   Coat the scallops with the spice paste and place over a medium barbecue, basting occasionally. Cook for 10 minutes, turning once, until tender, but do not overcook them.

7   Put the rocket, salad leaves and dressing in a bowl. Toss together well.

8   Serve the scallops hot, 2 skewers on each plate, with the salad.

Spiced Apricot Chicken

These spiced chicken legs are packed with dried apricots for an intense fruity flavour. The golden coating keeps the chicken moist and tender.

NUTRITIONAL INFORMATION

Calories ....305 Sugars 21g
Protein ....15g Fat 8g
Carbohydrate ...45g Saturates 1g

 10 mins   40 mins

SERVES 4

I N G R E D I E N T S

4 large, skinless chicken leg quarters

finely grated zest of 1 lemon

200 g/7 oz ready-to-eat dried apricots

1 tbsp ground cumin

1 tsp ground turmeric

125 ml/4 fl oz low-fat natural yogurt

salt and pepper

TO SERVE

250 g/9 oz brown rice

2 tbsp flaked hazelnuts, toasted

2 tbsp sunflower seeds, toasted

lemon wedges

fresh salad leaves

1 Remove any excess fat from the chicken legs. Carefully cut the flesh away from the thigh bone. Scrape the meat away down as far as the knuckle. Grasp the thigh bone firmly and twist it to break it away from the drumstick.

2 Open out the boned part of the chicken and sprinkle with lemon zest and pepper. Pack the dried apricots into each piece of chicken. Fold over to enclose, and secure with cocktail sticks.

3 Mix together the cumin, turmeric, yogurt, and salt and pepper, then brush over the chicken to coat evenly.

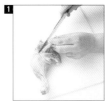

Place the chicken in an ovenproof dish and bake in a preheated oven, 190°C/375°F/Gas Mark 5, for 35–40 minutes or until the juices run clear when the chicken is pierced with a skewer.

4 Meanwhile, cook the rice in boiling, lightly salted water until just tender. Drain well. Stir in the hazelnuts and sunflower seeds. Serve the chicken with the rice, lemon wedges and salad leaves.

VARIATION

For a change, try using dried herbs instead of spices to flavour the coating. Use dried oregano, tarragon or rosemary – but remember dried herbs are more powerful than fresh, so you will need only a little.

Teppanyaki

This simple, Japanese style of cooking is ideal for thinly sliced breast of chicken. You can use thin turkey scallops, if you prefer.

NUTRITIONAL INFORMATION

Calories	206	Sugars	.........4g
Protein	.......30g	Fat	...........7g
Carbohydrate	....6g	Saturates	......2g

🍚 5 mins   🕐 10 mins

SERVES 4

INGREDIENTS

4 boneless chicken breasts

1 red pepper

1 green pepper

4 spring onions

8 baby corn cobs

100 g/3½ oz beansprouts

1 tbsp sesame or sunflower oil

4 tbsp soy sauce

4 tbsp mirin (see Cook's Tip, below)

1 tbsp grated fresh root ginger

1 Remove the skin from the chicken and slice the meat at a slight angle, to a thickness of about 5 mm/¼ inch.

2 Deseed and thinly slice the red and green peppers and trim and slice the spring onions and corn cobs.

3 Arrange the peppers, spring onions, corn cobs and beansprouts on a plate with the sliced chicken.

4 Heat a large ridged grill pan, then lightly brush with sesame or sunflower oil. Add the vegetables and chicken slices, in small batches, leaving enough space between them so that they cook thoroughly.

5 Put the soy sauce, mirin and ginger in a small serving bowl and stir together until combined. Serve as a dip with the chicken and vegetables.

COOK'S TIP

Mirin is a rich, sweet rice wine from Japan. You can buy it in Oriental shops, but if it is not available, add 1 tablespoon soft, light brown sugar to the sauce instead.

Lime Chicken Kebabs

These succulent chicken kebabs are coated in a sweet lime dressing and are served with a lime and mango relish. They make an ideal light meal.

NUTRITIONAL INFORMATION

Calories	199	Sugars	........14g
Protein	........28g	Fat	..........4g
Carbohydrate	...14g	Saturates	......1g

15 mins   10 mins

SERVES 4

INGREDIENTS

4 lean, boneless chicken breasts, skinned, about 125 g/4½ oz each

3 tbsp lime marmalade

1 tsp white wine vinegar

½ tsp lime zest, finely grated

1 tbsp lime juice

salt and pepper

TO SERVE

lime wedges

boiled white rice, sprinkled with chilli powder

SALSA

1 small mango

1 small red onion

1 tbsp lime juice

1 tbsp chopped fresh coriander

1 Slice the chicken breasts into thin pieces and thread onto 8 skewers so that the meat forms an S-shape down each skewer.

2 Preheat the grill to medium. Arrange the chicken kebabs on the grill rack. Mix together the lime marmalade, vinegar, lime zest and lime juice. Season with salt and pepper to taste. Brush the dressing generously over the chicken and grill for 5 minutes. Turn the chicken over, brush with the dressing again and grill for another 4-5 minutes until the chicken is cooked through.

3 Meanwhile, prepare the salsa. Peel the mango and slice the flesh off the smooth, central stone. Dice the flesh into small pieces and place in a small bowl.

4 Peel and finely chop the onion and mix into the mango together with the lime juice and chopped coriander. Season, cover and chill until required.

5 Serve the chicken kebabs with the salsa, accompanied by wedges of lime and boiled rice sprinkled with chilli powder.

COOK'S TIP

To prevent sticking, lightly oil metal skewers or dip bamboo skewers in water before threading the chicken onto them.

Cranberry Turkey Burgers

This recipe is bound to be popular with children and is very easy to prepare for their supper.

NUTRITIONAL INFORMATION

Calories	209	Sugars	. . . . .15g
Protein	. . . . .22g	Fat	. . . . .5g
Carbohydrate	. . .21g	Saturates	. . . . . .1g

45 mins   25 mins

SERVES 4

I N G R E D I E N T S

350 g/12 oz lean minced turkey

1 onion, finely chopped

1 tbsp chopped fresh sage

6 tbsp dry white breadcrumbs

4 tbsp cranberry sauce

1 egg white, lightly beaten

2 tsp sunflower oil

salt and pepper

TO SERVE

4 toasted wholemeal burger rolls

½ lettuce, shredded

4 tomatoes, sliced

4 tsp cranberry sauce

1 Combine the turkey, onion, sage, breadcrumbs and cranberry sauce in a bowl, and season to taste with salt and pepper. Mix in the egg white.

2 Using your hands, shape the mixture into four 10-cm/4-inch circles, about 2 cm/¾ inch thick. Chill for 30 minutes.

3 Line a grill rack with baking paper, making sure the ends are secured underneath the rack to ensure they do not catch fire. Place the burgers on top and brush lightly with oil. Put under a preheated moderate grill and cook for 10 minutes. Turn the burgers over and brush again with oil. Grill them for another 12–15 minutes until cooked through.

4 Fill each burger roll with lettuce, tomato and a burger and top with cranberry sauce.

COOK'S TIP

Look out for a variety of ready-minced meats at your butcher or supermarket. If unavailable, you can mince your own by choosing lean cuts and processing them in a blender or food processor.

Citrus Duckling Skewers

The tartness of citrus fruit goes well with the rich meat of duckling.
Duckling makes a delightful change from chicken for the barbecue.

NUTRITIONAL INFORMATION

Calories 205	Sugars 5g	
Protein 24g	Fat 10g	
Carbohydrate 5g	Saturates 2g	

15 mins, plus 30 mins marinating   20 mins

SERVES 12

INGREDIENTS

3 skinless boneless duckling breasts

1 small red onion, cut into wedges

1 small aubergine, cut into cubes

lime and lemon wedges, to garnish (optional)

MARINADE

grated zest and juice of 1 lemon

grated zest and juice of 1 lime

grated zest and juice of 1 orange

1 garlic clove, crushed

1 tsp dried oregano

2 tbsp olive oil

dash of Tabasco sauce

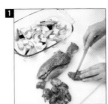

1 Cut the duckling into bite-sized pieces. Place in a non-metallic bowl with the prepared vegetables.

2 To make the marinade, put the lemon, lime and orange zest and juices in a screw-top jar with the garlic, oregano, oil and Tabasco. Shake until well combined. Pour the marinade over the duckling and vegetables and toss to coat. Set aside to marinate for 30 minutes.

3 Remove the duckling and vegetables from the marinade and thread them onto skewers, reserving the marinade.

4 Cook the skewers on an oiled rack over medium hot coals, turning and basting frequently with the reserved marinade, for 15-20 minutes until the meat is cooked through. Alternatively, cook under a preheated grill.

5 Serve the kebabs immediately, garnished with lime and lemon wedges for squeezing, if using.

COOK'S TIP

For more zing, add 1 teaspoon of chilli sauce to the marinade. The meat can be marinated for several hours, but it is best to marinate the vegetables separately for only about 30 minutes.

Italian Platter

This popular starter usually consists of vegetables soaked in olive oil and rich, creamy cheeses. Try this delicious low-fat version.

NUTRITIONAL INFORMATION

Calories	198	Sugars	........12g
Protein	........12g	Fat	..........6g
Carbohydrate	...25g	Saturates	......3g

🅖 🅖

🍲 10 mins   🕐 0 mins

SERVES 4

I N G R E D I E N T S

125 g/4½ oz reduced-fat mozzarella cheese, drained

60 g/2¼ oz lean Parma ham

400 g/14 oz canned artichoke hearts, drained

4 ripe figs

1 small mango

few plain grissini (bread sticks), to serve

D R E S S I N G

1 small orange

1 tbsp passata

1 tsp wholegrain mustard

4 tbsp low-fat natural yogurt

fresh basil leaves

salt and pepper

1 Cut the cheese into 12 sticks, 6.5 cm/2½ inches long. Remove the fat from the Parma ham and slice the meat into 12 strips. Carefully wrap a strip of meat around each stick of cheese and arrange neatly on a serving platter.

2 Halve the artichoke hearts and cut the figs into quarters. Arrange them on the serving platter in groups.

3 Peel the mango, then slice it down each side of the large, flat, central stone. Slice the mango into strips and arrange them so that they form a fan shape on the serving platter.

4 To make the dressing, use a vegetable peeler to pare the rind from half of the orange. Cut the rind into small strips and place them in a bowl. Extract the juice from the orange and add it to the bowl containing the rind.

5 Add the passata, mustard, yogurt and seasoning to the bowl and mix together. Shred the basil leaves and mix them into the dressing.

6 Spoon the dressing into a small dish and serve with the Italian Platter, accompanied by grissini.

VARIATION

For a change, serve this dish with a French stick or an Italian bread, widely available from supermarkets, and use it to soak up the delicious dressing.

Pork & Apple Skewers

Flavoured with mustard and served with a mustard sauce, these kebabs make an ideal lunch or they can be served as part of a barbecued meal.

NUTRITIONAL INFORMATION

Calories 290   Sugars 11g
Protein . . . . .24g   Fat 17g
Carbohydrate . . . .11g   Saturates 5g

10 mins   15 mins

SERVES 4

I N G R E D I E N T S

450 g/1 lb pork fillet

2 eating apples

a little lemon juice

1 lemon

2 tsp wholegrain mustard

2 tsp Dijon mustard

2 tbsp apple or orange juice

2 tbsp sunflower oil

crusty brown bread, to serve

M U S T A R D   S A U C E

1 tbsp wholegrain mustard

1 tsp Dijon mustard

6 tbsp single cream

1 To make the mustard sauce, combine the wholegrain and Dijon mustards in a small bowl and slowly blend in the cream. Set aside while you prepare the pork and apple skewers.

2 Cut the pork fillet into bite-sized pieces and set aside until required.

3 Core the apples, then cut them into thick wedges. Toss the apple wedges in a little lemon juice – this will prevent any discoloration. Cut the lemon into fairly thin slices.

4 Thread the pork, apple and lemon slices alternately onto 4 skewers.

5 In a bowl, mix together the mustards, fruit juice and oil until well combined. Brush the mixture over the kebabs and cook them over hot coals for about 10–15 minutes, turning and basting frequently with the mustard marinade.

6 Transfer the kebabs to warm serving plates and spoon a little of the mustard sauce on top. Serve hot with crusty brown bread.

Tangy Pork Fillet

Barbecued until tender in a parcel of foil, these tasty pork slices are served with a tangy orange sauce.

NUTRITIONAL INFORMATION

Calories	230	Sugars 16g
Protein	........19g	Fat 9g
Carbohydrate	...20g	Saturates 3g

10 mins   50 mins

SERVES 4

INGREDIENTS

400 g/14 oz lean pork fillet

3 tbsp orange marmalade

grated zest and juice of 1 orange

1 tbsp white wine vinegar

dash of Tabasco sauce

salt and pepper

SAUCE

1 tbsp olive oil

1 small onion, chopped

1 small green pepper, deseeded and
    thinly sliced

1 tbsp cornflour

150 ml/5 fl oz orange juice

TO SERVE

freshly cooked rice

fresh mixed salad leaves

1 Place a large piece of double-thickness foil in a shallow dish. Put the pork fillet in the centre of the foil and season to taste.

2 Heat the marmalade, orange zest and juice, vinegar and Tabasco sauce in a small pan, stirring, until the marmalade melts and the ingredients combine. Pour the mixture over the pork and wrap the meat in the foil. Seal the parcel well so that the juices cannot run out. Place over hot coals and barbecue for 25 minutes, turning the parcel occasionally.

3 For the sauce, heat the oil in a pan and cook the onion for 2–3 minutes. Add the pepper and cook for 3–4 minutes.

4 Remove the pork from the foil and place on the rack. Pour the juices into the pan with the sauce.

5 Continue barbecuing the pork for another 10–20 minutes, turning, until cooked through and golden.

6 In a bowl, mix the cornflour into a paste with a little orange juice. Add to the sauce with the remaining cooking juices and orange juice. Cook, stirring, until it thickens. Slice the pork, spoon over the sauce and serve with freshly cooked rice and fresh salad leaves.

Ginger Beef with Chilli

Serve these fruity, hot and spicy steaks with noodles. Use a non-stick ridged grill pan to cook with a minimum of fat.

NUTRITIONAL INFORMATION

Calories	179	Sugars	.........8g
Protein	........21g	Fat	...........6g
Carbohydrate	....8g	Saturates	......2g

15 mins, plus 30 mins marinating   10 mins

SERVES 4

I N G R E D I E N T S

4 lean beef steaks (such as rump, sirloin or fillet), about 100 g/3½ oz each

2 tbsp ginger wine

2.5-cm/1-inch piece fresh root ginger, finely chopped

1 garlic clove, crushed

1 tsp ground chilli

1 tsp vegetable oil

salt and pepper

red chilli strips, to garnish

TO SERVE

2 spring onions, shredded

freshly cooked noodles

RELISH

225 g/8 oz fresh pineapple

1 small red pepper

1 red chilli

2 tbsp light soy sauce

1 piece stem ginger in syrup, drained and chopped

1 Trim any excess fat from the beef if necessary. Using a meat mallet or covered rolling pin, pound the steaks until they are approximately 1 cm/½ inch thick. Season on both sides and place in a shallow dish.

2 Mix the ginger wine, chopped ginger, garlic and chilli in a bowl and pour over the meat. Cover and marinate in the refrigerator for 30 minutes.

3 Meanwhile, make the relish. Peel and finely chop the pineapple and place it in a bowl. Halve, deseed and finely chop the red pepper and chilli. Stir into the pineapple together with the soy sauce and stem ginger. Cover and chill until required.

4 Brush a ridged grill pan with the oil and heat until very hot. Drain the steaks and add to the pan, pressing down to sear. Lower the heat and cook for 5 minutes. Turn the steaks over and cook for an additional 5 minutes.

5 Drain the steaks on kitchen paper and transfer to serving plates. Garnish with chilli strips and serve with shredded spring onions, the relish and freshly cooked noodles.

Pan-fried Liver with Thyme

This tasty dish is very simple to make. You can use either calf's or lamb's liver for the main ingredient.

NUTRITIONAL INFORMATION

Calories	462	Sugars	.........1g
Protein	........27g	Fat	..........31g
Carbohydrate	...14g	Saturates	......6g

5 mins   10 mins

SERVES 1

I N G R E D I E N T S

1 slice calf's liver, about 125 g/4½ oz, or
  2 smaller slices, or 2 slices lamb's liver

1 tbsp seasoned flour

2 tsp oil

1 tbsp margarine or butter

2 tbsp white wine

½ tsp chopped fresh thyme or a large pinch
  of dried thyme

pinch of finely grated lime or lemon zest

2 tsp lemon juice

1 tsp capers

1–2 tbsp single cream (optional)

salt and pepper

TO GARNISH

lemon or lime slices

fresh thyme or parsley

TO SERVE

boiled new potatoes

fresh salad leaves

1   Trim the liver if necessary and then toss it in the seasoned flour until evenly coated.

2   Heat the oil and margarine in a frying pan. When foaming, add the liver and cook for 2–3 minutes on each side until well sealed and just cooked through. Take care not to overcook or the liver will become tough and hard. Transfer to a plate and keep warm.

3   Add the wine, 1 tablespoon of water, the thyme, citrus rind, lemon juice, capers and seasoning to the pan juices and heat through gently until bubbling and syrupy. Add the cream, if using, and reheat gently. Adjust the seasoning and spoon the sauce over the liver.

4   Garnish the liver with lemon or lime slices, and thyme or parsley, and serve with new potatoes and a salad.

Lamb & Tomato Koftas

These little meatballs, served with a minty yogurt dressing, can be prepared in advance, ready to cook when required.

NUTRITIONAL INFORMATION

Calories	183	Sugars	.........5g
Protein	........15g	Fat	..........11g
Carbohydrate	....5g	Saturates	......4g

15 mins   10 mins

SERVES 4

INGREDIENTS

225 g/8 oz finely minced lean lamb

1½ onions, peeled

1–2 garlic cloves, crushed

1 dried red chilli, finely chopped (optional)

2–3 tsp garam masala

2 tbsp chopped fresh mint

2 tsp lemon juice

salt

2 tbsp vegetable oil

4 small tomatoes, cut into quarters

sprigs of fresh mint, to garnish

YOGURT DRESSING

150 ml/5 fl oz low-fat natural yogurt

5-cm/2-inch piece cucumber, grated

2 tbsp chopped fresh mint

½ tsp cumin seeds, toasted (optional)

1 Place the minced lamb in a bowl. Finely chop 1 onion and add to the bowl with the garlic, and chilli if using. Stir in the garam masala, mint and lemon juice and season well with salt. Mix well.

2 Divide the mixture in half, then divide each half into 10 equal portions and form each into a small ball. Roll the balls in the oil to coat. Cut the remaining onion half into quarters and separate into layers.

3 Thread 5 of the spicy meatballs, 4 tomato quarters and some of the onion layers alternately onto each of 4 metal or presoaked bamboo skewers so that they are evenly distributed.

4 Brush the vegetables with the remaining oil and cook the koftas under a hot grill for about 10 minutes, turning frequently, until they are browned all over and cooked through.

5 Meanwhile, prepare the yogurt dressing for the koftas. In a small bowl, mix together the yogurt, grated cucumber, mint, and toasted cumin seeds, if using.

6 Garnish the lamb and tomato koftas with mint sprigs and place on a large serving platter. Serve the koftas hot with the yogurt dressing.

Hotpot Chops

A hotpot is a meat casserole, made with carrots and onions and a potato topping. This dish makes an interesting alternative.

NUTRITIONAL INFORMATION

Calories 250	Sugars 2g
Protein 27g	Fat 12g
Carbohydrate 8g	Saturates 5g

 10 mins   30 mins

SERVES 4

I N G R E D I E N T S

4 lean, boneless lamb leg steaks, about
125 g/4½ oz each

1 small onion, thinly sliced

1 carrot, thinly sliced

1 potato, thinly sliced

1 tsp olive oil

1 tsp dried rosemary

salt and pepper

fresh rosemary, to garnish

freshly steamed green vegetables, to serve

1 Preheat the oven to 180°C/350°F/Gas Mark 4. Using a sharp knife, trim any excess fat from the lamb steaks.

2 Season both sides of the steaks with salt and pepper and arrange them on a baking tray.

3 Alternate layers of sliced onion, carrot and potato on top of each lamb steak.

4 Brush the tops of the potato lightly with oil. Season well with salt and pepper to taste and then sprinkle with a little dried rosemary.

5 Bake the steaks in the oven for 25–30 minutes until the lamb is tender and cooked through.

6 Remove the lamb from the oven and transfer to warmed serving plates.

7 Garnish with fresh rosemary and serve accompanied by a selection of steamed green vegetables.

VARIATION

This recipe would work equally well with boneless chicken breasts. Pound the chicken slightly with a meat mallet or covered rolling pin so that the pieces are the same thickness throughout.

Lamb with a Spice Crust

Lamb neck fillets are tender cuts that are not too thick and are, therefore, ideal for cooking on the barbecue.

NUTRITIONAL INFORMATION

Calories	203	Sugars	.........9g
Protein	........16g	Fat	..........10g
Carbohydrate	...12g	Saturates	......4g

 5 mins   45 mins

SERVES 4

I N G R E D I E N T S

1 tbsp olive oil, plus extra for greasing

2 tbsp light muscovado sugar

2 tbsp wholegrain mustard

1 tbsp horseradish sauce

1 tbsp plain flour

350 g/12 oz neck fillets of lamb

salt and pepper

TO SERVE

coleslaw

slices of tomato

1 Combine the oil, sugar, mustard, horseradish sauce, flour, and salt and pepper to taste in a shallow, non-metallic dish until they are well mixed.

2 Roll the lamb in the spice mixture until well coated.

COOK'S TIP

If preferred, the lamb can be completely removed from the foil for the second part of the cooking. Cook the lamb directly over the coals for a smokier barbecue flavour, basting with extra oil if necessary.

3 Lightly oil one or two pieces of foil or a large, double thickness of foil. Place the lamb on the foil and wrap it up so that the meat is completely enclosed.

4 Place the foil parcel over hot coals for 30 minutes, turning the parcel over occasionally to cook evenly.

5 Carefully open the foil parcel, spoon the cooking juices over the spiced

lamb and continue barbecuing for another 10–15 minutes or until the meat is completely cooked through.

6 Place the lamb on a platter and remove the foil. Cut into thick slices and serve with coleslaw and tomato slices.

Chocolate & Pineapple Cake

Decorated with thick yogurt and canned pineapple, this is a low-fat cake, but it is by no means lacking in flavour.

NUTRITIONAL INFORMATION

Calories 199	Sugars 19g	
Protein 5g	Fat 9g	
Carbohydrate . . .28g	Saturates 3g	

10 mins   25 mins

SERVES 9

I N G R E D I E N T S

150 g/5½ oz low-fat spread, plus extra for greasing

125 g/4½ oz caster sugar

100 g/3½ oz self-raising flour, sifted

3 tbsp cocoa powder, sifted

1½ tsp baking powder

2 eggs

225 g/8 oz canned pineapple pieces in natural juice

125 ml/4 fl oz low-fat thick natural yogurt

about 1 tbsp icing sugar

grated chocolate, to decorate

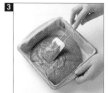

1 Lightly grease a 20-cm/8-inch square cake tin with a little low-fat spread.

2 Put the remaining low-fat spread in a large mixing bowl with the caster sugar, flour, cocoa powder, baking powder and eggs, then beat together with a wooden spoon or an electric hand whisk until smooth.

3 Pour the cake mixture into the prepared tin and level the surface. Bake in a preheated oven, 190°C/375°F/Gas Mark 5, for 20–25 minutes or until springy to the touch. Cool slightly in the tin, then transfer to a wire rack to cool completely.

4 Drain the pineapple, chop the pineapple pieces and drain again.

Reserve a little pineapple for decoration. Put the remainder into a bowl with the yogurt and stir together. Sweeten to taste with icing sugar.

5 Spread the pineapple and yogurt mixture over the cake and decorate with the reserved pineapple pieces. Sprinkle over the grated chocolate.

Mixed Fruit Brûlées

Traditionally a rich mixture made with double cream, this fruit-based version is just as tempting using single cream and low-fat yogurt.

NUTRITIONAL INFORMATION

Calories 165   Sugars 21g
Protein . . . . .5g   Fat 7g
Carbohydrate . . .21g   Saturates 5g

 5 mins   5 mins

SERVES 4

I N G R E D I E N T S

450 g/1 lb prepared assorted summer fruits, such as strawberries, raspberries, blackcurrants, redcurrants and cherries, thawed if frozen

150 ml/5 fl oz single cream

150 ml/5 fl oz low-fat natural yogurt

1 tsp vanilla extract

4 tbsp Demerara sugar

1 Divide the prepared strawberries, raspberries, blackcurrants, redcurrants and cherries evenly among 4 small, heatproof ramekins.

2 Combine the cream, yogurt and vanilla extract.

3 Spoon the mixture over the fruit to cover it completely.

4 Top each serving with 1 tablespoon of Demerara sugar and place the desserts under a preheated grill for 2–3 minutes until the sugar melts and begins to caramelise. Set aside for a couple of minutes before serving.

COOK'S TIP

Look out for half-fat creams, in single and double varieties. They are good substitutes for occasional use. Alternatively, in this recipe, double the quantity of yogurt for a lower-fat version.

Tropical Fruit Fool

Fruit fools are always popular, and this light, tangy version will be no exception. You can use your favourite fruits in this recipe.

NUTRITIONAL INFORMATION

Calories ....149 Sugars 25g
Protein ....6g Fat 0.4g
Carbohydrate ...32g Saturates 0.2g

 35 mins   🕐 0 mins

SERVES 4

INGREDIENTS

1 medium ripe mango

2 kiwi fruit

1 medium banana

2 tbsp lime juice

½ tsp finely grated lime zest, plus extra
   to decorate

2 egg whites

425 g/15 oz canned low-fat custard

½ tsp vanilla extract

2 passion fruit

1   Peel the mango, then slice either side of the smooth, flat, central stone. Roughly chop the flesh and process in a food processor or blender until smooth. Alternatively, mash with a fork.

2   Peel the kiwi fruit, then chop the flesh into small pieces and place in a bowl. Peel and cut the banana crossways into small slices and add to the bowl. Toss the fruit in the lime juice and lime zest and mix well.

3   In a grease-free bowl, whisk the egg whites until stiff and then gently fold in the custard and vanilla extract until thoroughly mixed.

4   In 4 serving glasses, alternately layer the chopped fruit, mango purée and custard mixture, finishing with the custard on top. Set aside to chill in the refrigerator for 20 minutes.

5   Halve the passion fruit. Using a small spoon, scoop out the seeds and spoon the passion fruit over the fruit fools. Decorate each serving with the extra lime zest and serve.

VARIATION

Other tropical fruit purées to try include papaya, with chopped pineapple and dates or pomegranate seeds to decorate.